TAROT

TAROT

DIVINATION, WISDOM & SELF-DISCOVERY

NIKKI JAY

This pocket illustrated edition first published in 2025 by
Amber Books Ltd
United House
North Road
London N7 9DP
United Kingdom

www.amberbooks.co.uk
Facebook: amberbooks
YouTube: amberbooksltd
Instagram: amberbooksltd
X(Twitter): @amberbooks

Copyright © 2025 Amber Books Ltd

All rights reserved. No part of this work may be reproduced,
stored in a retrieval system, or transmitted in any form or by
any means, electronic, mechanical, photocopying, recording,
or otherwise, without the prior permission of the copyright holder.

ISBN: 978-1-83886-585-6

Printed in China

Project Editors: Michael Spilling and Anna Brownbridge
Picture Research: Terry Forshaw
Design: Rick Fawcett and Mark Batley

CONTENTS

୬୧

6
INTRODUCTION

12
THE MAJOR ARCANA

102
THE MINOR ARCANA

224
PICTURE CREDITS

Introduction

Tarot cards have been used by mystics, seers, witches, fortune tellers and even the royal court for centuries. No one knows exactly where they first derived from. This has been a point of discussion among historians and tarot experts for many years. Some believe tarot cards originated in the Far East, others in India, and they were brought to Europe around the early Middle Ages. Even the word 'tarot' has proved contentious in its origin.
What has been agreed upon though, is that the Rider-Waite deck changed the face of tarot forever. Many decks today are based on the original Rider-Waite and this is the deck you will find used in this book.

The tarot deck

Whatever its origin, tarot has changed very little since the 15th century. The tarot deck is made up of 78 cards – 22 Major Arcana and 56 Lesser, or Minor Arcana.

The Major Arcana contains the 'trump' cards. These are the more powerful of the deck, from the Fool at 0 through to the World at 21, although even this is a point of contention, some tarot experts place the Fool at the beginning, some at the end and some in the middle.

MINOR ARCANA
The Minor Arcana, sometimes known as Lesser Arcana, are the suit cards in a cartomantic tarot deck.

CUPS　　　　PENTACLES　　　　SWORDS　　　　WANDS

The Major Arcana represents the fundamental energies of life itself – our issues, motivations and core values. These cards are used to represent both the individual and society as a whole. These are the deep psychological and sociological issues of the conscious and unconscious mind.

The Minor Arcana contains four suits, much like a regular deck of cards. These are Cups, Pentacles, Swords and Wands. Each of the suits contains numbered cards from Ace through to 10, and then four court cards: Page, Knight, Queen and King.

The Minor Arcana cards are used to navigate through daily life experiences. The court cards will represent personalities you may come into contact with and how these affect your daily existence, or your own character traits.

Tarot allows you to consider a problem, give a voice to it, work it through and see where the blocks might be.

FIVE CARD SPREAD

4.

5.

1.

2.

3.

1. This card is your recent past, either what has just happened or what you are currently experiencing.
2. This is the current influence, and is your situation right now.
3. This card represents what is about to unfold and is therefore the 'future' card.
4. The fourth card gives you some advice about what action you may need to take based on what your spirit guides think is best for you.
5. This is the most likely outcome based on things as they are now. You always have the power to change the direction you are going and change this outcome if you don't like it.

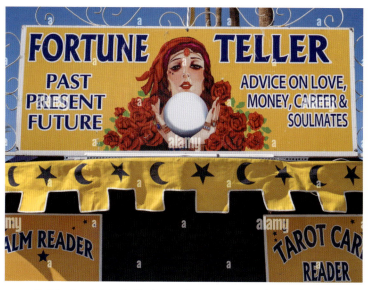

Traditional carnival stand selling fortune telling, palm reading and tarot card services at a fair in Southern California, USA

The Rider-Waite-Smith tarot deck

This deck should really be called the Smith-Waite tarot deck as its two creators were Arthur Edward Waite and Pamela Colman Smith. Rider was the British publishing house that published the deck in 1910. Arthur Waite was the creator of the deck – it was his conception – but Pamela Colman Smith was the artist. It is not clear how much free rein she had over the artwork, but looking at the text from Arthur Waite, it is likely that she is the reason that the Minor Arcana had such a makeover.

Both Arthur and Pamela were members of The Order Of The Golden Dawn and they worked together to create this new version of the tarot that we all recognise today. The biggest change was that the Minor Arcana now had scenes on every card, rather than the initial geometric designs that previous versions had.

Quick tips to get you started

Although this is not a 'how to' tarot book, I will include a couple of tips for you to get you started. If you want a more in-depth guide on how to read tarot, there are many books available. Try drawing a card a day to see what your day holds for you. Really study it, see how you feel, use the pictures to dig deep and trust your intuition. Then read the meaning and see how you can relate it to your question.

You can do a simple three-card spread, where the first card represents your (recent) past, the second is the present and the final one is the possible future outcome. This is a very easy spread to help you get to know the cards.

Whatever spread you choose, just be clear about the question you are asking. Yes/no questions are very restrictive, so try to avoid those if you want to dig deep. Think how you can relate the card to your question. Does it represent someone you know? What issues does it bring up? Are you excited by the possibility? Ask lots of questions about how it makes you feel.

Tarot is all about gaining insight into your deepest self, working out where you may be blocked and finding ways to navigate through life's ups and downs. So just relax and feel your way into it.

Enjoy!

Selecting tarot cards from the deck.

CELTIC CROSS TAROT SPREAD

1. This is you.
2. This crosses you.
3. This crowns you.
4. This is beneath you.
5. This is behind you.
6. This is before you.
7. Your attitude.
8. People influencing you.
9. Your hopes and fears
10. Outcome.

THE MAJOR ARCANA

The Major Arcana are the named cards
in a cartomantic tarot pack. There are usually
22 such cards in a standard 78-card pack

Far left: The Hanged Man
Middle left: The High Priestess
Near left: The Lovers

MAJOR ARCANA

0.
THE FOOL

A character full of hope and expectation, the Fool is childlike and sometimes a little naive, looking forwards to new beginnings with anticipation of what is to come without fear. The Fool is willing to take a leap of faith, even with a dog yapping at their heels, warning them that they are about to walk off a cliff. The Fool carries their possessions in a sack slung over their shoulder, without a care in the world.

INTERPRETATIONS

UPRIGHT

When the Fool appears in a reading, it is there to show you that it is time for a bold move. Take a leap of faith and trust your instincts and your knowledge. Know that you have the ability to start something, or to start over, with a fresh perspective. Expect the unexpected, be ready for an adventure and take your enthusiasm with you. But don't be careless or reckless, still use your head and listen to sound advice.

REVERSED

A reminder to not be foolish, don't leap before you look. Be aware of the risks you are taking and do your research. It can also show that your own fears are holding you back. If you have done your due diligence and you have the information you need, be bold and take the first steps.

MAJOR ARCANA

1.
THE MAGICIAN

The Magician is all about personal
power. He directs magic from a higher
realm through the wand he holds
aloft and directs it, through his finger,
into the earth to create his desires.
He has the ability to manipulate
all the elements and is a master of
manifestation. He is the alchemist,
using all the elements of wands, swords,
pentacles and cups to create
the desired outcome.

INTERPRETATIONS

UPRIGHT

When the Magician appears in a reading he is a reminder that you have the ability to manifest your desires and it is time for you to reach your potential. He is all about mastery, focus and belief in yourself. Know that you don't have all the answers but expect opportunities that seem magical and be prepared to take them.

REVERSED

When reversed, it is a sign that you may feel blocked, that your power is somehow lacking. You may not believe you have the ability to achieve what you want and are looking to others for the answers. It can also indicate there is a person in your vicinity who is not trustworthy.

The Magician from the 78-card Marseille set.

MAJOR ARCANA

2.

THE HIGH PRIESTESS

The High Priestess sits between two pillars with a veil hiding what is behind her. This shows the hidden knowledge she has – and our inability to understand it. She guards the secrets of the unconscious and unknown between the real world and all other realms. When you draw this card, it is time to look behind the veil of illusion to discover what is currently being hidden.

INTERPRETATIONS

UPRIGHT

When the High Priestess appears in a reading she is there to remind you to dig deep to see that which is not obvious. Listen to your intuition and trust your instincts. If something feels off, it probably isn't worth pursuing. It is time to connect with the divine to unlock the secrets you need to know.

REVERSED

The High Priestess shows up in the reverse as a warning that you are neglecting your own instincts, putting too much trust in others and not paying attention to what your gut is trying to tell you. This blocked energy can be released through connectivity to the divine; try meditation.

MAJOR ARCANA

3.

THE EMPRESS

The Empress is divine feminine energy. She represents love, a luxurious life, fertility and creativity. Her appearance may indicate that this is a time of great growth. She is the archetype of abundance and feminine power. She is the ultimate mother figure, nurturing, caring and compassionate. For me, she represents Mother Earth herself.

INTERPRETATIONS

UPRIGHT

This card indicates that you are beginning a phase of great growth and achievement. Keep nurturing your project to achieve your goal. It is also a reminder that you can ask for help if you need it. In love she may represent the need to nurture yourself and others. She can be a sign that you are entering a fertile period and pregnancy may be on the cards.

REVERSED

You may be smothering your loved ones at this time. It is time to take a step back and let go of some of the controlling issues you have. It can also indicate that you are putting your efforts into the wrong areas or people, which is blocking your growth. She can also represent difficulties with a mother figure.

MAJOR ARCANA

4.
THE EMPEROR

The Emperor is the King of the cards, divine masculine energy, the boss man. The Emperor represents power and leadership and is the father figure. He is the strategist and is the one who establishes the rules and uses his position to control any situation. He is assertive and thrives on structure to create stability. I also think of him as the ultimate entrepreneur.

INTERPRETATIONS

UPRIGHT

When The Emperor appears he is encouraging you to embrace your own power, whether that is taking control in your career or your love life. He is all about direction. Establish what you want and go for it in a strategic way. Set healthy boundaries where needed and use your personal power for your highest good. Believe in yourself, take action and success will follow.

REVERSED

You may be trying too hard: effort without direction can lead to procrastination. You may be feeling less than at your best, neglecting yourself and creating an imbalance that leads to a feeling of powerlessness. It is time to focus your efforts and regain some balance in your life.

The Emperor from the 78-card Marseille set.

MAJOR ARCANA

5.

THE HIEROPHANT

The Hierophant represent rules and regulations. He is all about honouring tradition and controlling your life through predictability and balance – an antithesis to chaos. He is the religious, spiritual and educational leader sharing his knowledge, guiding you through ritual and spiritual practices. With this card, your spiritual soul needs nurturing and a way to express itself.

INTERPRETATIONS

UPRIGHT

If the Hierophant shows up in a reading it may be that you are being advised to follow conventional wisdom and to not upset the status quo. You are being encouraged to seek help from a spiritual leader or wise elder to help you reach your goals. It is also an indicator of personal spiritual growth and learning to pick your battles.

REVERSED

You may have become so stuck in your own beliefs that you are stunting your own personal growth. Although following the rules is good in some circumstances, sometimes it is advised that you follow your intuition and use a degree of common sense. Also don't ignore traditional wisdom, it may serve you yet.

The Lovers

MAJOR ARCANA

6.
THE LOVERS

The Lovers can represent a union of two people in love. It can also represent two separate entities that are trying to become one. But this card used to be called the Choice for a very good reason. It is about your power to decide which path you want to take. The key thing about the choice you make is that it should be done from a place of love. Choose the thing that really resonates with your soul.

INTERPRETATIONS

UPRIGHT

In a love reading, the Lovers indicates a romantic union through mutual attraction. It can also mean that you have to decide between two possible suitors. It may also show that marriage, or taking a relationship to the next level, is possible at this time. For your career, you may be facing an important decision. The advice, whether about love, career or personal growth, is to choose that which speaks to your heart's desire.

REVERSED

You may be feeling some sense of loss or regret over a decision you have made recently, or a literal loss of someone or something that you loved dearly. It can indicate you are dogmatically ignoring your heart, choosing to make decisions based on what you perceive as logic, or because it is expected. You are being encouraged to look at what love means to you.

The Lovers from the 78-card Marseille set.

MAJOR ARCANA

7.

THE CHARIOT

The Chariot shows two sphinxes, one black, one white, facing in opposite directions. The chariot driver's job is to control them and get them both pulling in the same direction. In other words, control, will power and a strong sense of purpose are needed here.
This is a card of victory and success coupled with forward momentum.

INTERPRETATIONS

UPRIGHT

The power lays in your motivation when you draw this card. Your intention is everything. Get clear on what you want and avoid distractions and you will find yourself charging forward and achieving your goals. Whether love, career or personal growth is the desire, this card represents the opportunity to get what you want with perseverance and tenacity.

REVERSED

You may have lost your focus and the result is the sphinxes are pulling hard in opposite directions, preventing you from moving forwards. Or you may feel as if you are galloping headlong into something you don't want and you run the risk of crashing. Whether you feel stuck or like you're going the wrong way, you need to regain control or your progress will remain blocked.

MAJOR ARCANA

8.
STRENGTH

The Strength card shows a lion being petted by a woman, depicting strength with compassion. This is rarely about physical strength, unless that is your enquiry. It is more concerned with inner strength, tenacity and the ability to overcome any obstacles in your life. It also reminds us to be gentle with ourselves and others. It is not concerned with aggressiveness but with quiet contemplative self-assurance.

INTERPRETATIONS

UPRIGHT

When you draw the Strength card in a reading it shows that even though you may feel nervous about a situation, you have the inner conviction to deal with it. With self-discipline and gentle nudges in the right direction, you will achieve your goal. You cannot force the matter, but how you react is key. Be prepared to forgive others and approach things calmly. It is time for some self-awareness.

REVERSED

You may be trying to force a situation or bend someone else to your will instead of allowing things to unfold naturally. You may be lacking trust in your own ability or in the universe to provide what is needed. This could backfire and cause more problems than it solves. Compassion is key, along with some self-reliance.

Strength from the 78-card Marseille set.

MAJOR ARCANA

9.
THE HERMIT

The Hermit shows a figure alone in a long robe, holding a staff and a lantern. This figure is a wise old sage who spends his days alone, searching for answers with a sense of introspection and self reflection. He stands for calm, guidance and inner peace. When called on, The Hermit is the wise guide who will give you the help you need.

INTERPRETATIONS

UPRIGHT

When the Hermit is pulled in a reading, he shows a need for some quiet time, often alone, to reflect and look for answers from within. You may need some inner healing, or just to find a way to balance your life. It is time to take a deep look at your current life, career or love-life to discover whether you feel truly fulfilled. It is a process worth taking your time over, and its sometimes wise to consult an expert.

REVERSED

Although taking time for yourself can be hugely beneficial and healing, be careful not to isolate yourself. You may be spending too much time alone and this can be detrimental to your mental health. The company of others could be the tonic you need right now to get you out of a funk.

MAJOR ARCANA

10.
WHEEL OF FORTUNE

The Wheel of Fortune represents the inevitability of change. It is a cycle, always moving through the highs and lows of life. As it is fortune's wheel, it does point to luck, destiny and divine timing. But nothing is certain in life except uncertainty and nothing is constant except change. When the Wheel of Fortune shows up, you can be certain that you are about to make a move in life.

INTERPRETATIONS

UPRIGHT

When the Wheel of Fortune shows up in a reading it often signifies that fortune is in your favour. You may be lucky in love and find things just seem to be happening in your favour. Chance meetings or circumstances bring new opportunities with your career. You may find yourself achieving your goals more quickly than expected. If you have been in a slump, remember that the wheel keeps turning and that is about to change.

REVERSED

You may feel stuck, like the wheel can't move forwards. You may have experienced some disappointments or unlucky events that have left you feeling blocked. If things aren't turning out the way you think they should, remember the message of this card is that the wheel keeps on turning. Nothing is permanent and things will turn in your favour again.

MAJOR ARCANA

11.
JUSTICE

Justice depicts a figure sitting on a thrown with the scales of justice in one hand and a sword in the other. I think of it as the sword of truth, it is an emblem of wisdom and action. This card represents balance, fairness and right decisions being made. It is time to look at things from all sides to come to an honest and unemotional conclusion. The right outcome will occur, whether that is to reward or punish.

INTERPRETATIONS

UPRIGHT

When asking about your career, Justice shows that you may need to be cautious, you may be facing criticism. There may be a need to weigh up the pros and cons of an opportunity. In love, balance is needed. In all circumstances, taking a step back and looking at things from a non-emotional standpoint will help. But know that Justice will deliver the right outcome, which is usually in your favour.

REVERSED

You may feel like someone is getting away with more than they should, that there is some sort of injustice. Someone may be wrongly accused of something. Look at it from a logical point of view, are you being judgmental? Also, you may be being taken advantage of by others so it's time to set your boundaries and not let the emotions of a situation sway you.

Justice from the Tarocchi Cards of Mantegna.

MAJOR ARCANA

12.
THE HANGED MAN

The Hanged Man represents paradox. He puts himself in a state of limbo because it is time to take a step back. Sometimes the only action required is no action, but rather trust. Trust yourself and the universe. The paradox comes in as sometimes you are required to do the opposite of what you think you should be doing. It is like solving a cryptic puzzle when you don't have all the clues.

INTERPRETATIONS

UPRIGHT

When the Hanged Man shows up in a reading he is there to remind you that a new perspective is needed. There is something that you need to work out and right now, the best course of action is to wait. If you can let go of control and trust that things will work out, then you will find yourself getting to where you want to be a lot more quickly. It is time to look at things from all angles and not force the situation.

REVERSED

You may be holding onto the sense of control far too tightly and this is causing you more problems than it is solving. Refusing to let go may become detrimental to your well-being. If you are refusing to see things from a different perspective, it may be out of fear. This only serves to keep you in a state of victimhood.

MAJOR ARCANA

13.
DEATH

Death can seem like a scary card to draw, but it very rarely relates to a mortal death. Think of it as more of a transformational energy, something must come to an end in order for something new to begin. The Death card embodies change, the chance for a reset, a make-over. It is the symbol of release, purging something from your life that no longer serves you, to make way for something better. It is actually a very positive card.

INTERPRETATIONS

UPRIGHT

If Death shows up in a reading, you can expect that some aspect of your life is coming to a conclusion. It could mean a relationship ending, a lost job or just shifting gears in some way. But out of that ending you can look forward to something better. So don't resist the change, it is not always something drastic. Go with it and look forward to what is to come. It is a positive!

REVERSED

When reversed this shows that you may be resisting a necessary change that is preventing you from moving forward. If you are grieving over the loss of something you may feel a great sense of lack. Remember, change happens, it is inevitable, so don't prolong your suffering.

MAJOR ARCANA

14.
TEMPERANCE

The angel of Temperance is all about balance, with one foot in water and the other on land, signifying the need for staying grounded while also going with the flow. Temperance has two cups and is pouring the water between them, signifying the bringing together of separate energies into one. It is all about finding the right mix of elements that work for you, with patience, compromise and moderation.

INTERPRETATIONS

UPRIGHT

It is time for you to work out the way to merge the energies in your life to find balance. I always like to think of Temperance as a way of playing with energy to find your equilibrium in any area of your life. Patience will be needed at this time, with yourself and others, but remember, you are creating something that is unique and wonderful for you. Try to strike that sense of moderation that will help you to thrive as you move forwards.

REVERSED

When Temperance is reversed, this indicates that there may be a tipping of the balance that is impacting you negatively. You may find you have too much or too little of what you need. It can also indicate that the two elements you are trying to bring together are just not meant to be at this time.

MAJOR ARCANA

15.
THE DEVIL

You can see the two people bound to one another with chains and the Devil appears to be in control. The Devil represents unhealthy bonds, addictive behaviours, temptation and toxic relationships. But the Devil reflects our own inner darkness, the Devil within. The Devil asks us to accept our own limitations and develop a sense of self awareness. It's other's expectations that are holding us back and our belief in them.

INTERPRETATIONS

UPRIGHT

On the positive side, the Devil can represent a firm commitment, a lasting contract that can't be easily broken. As they say though, the Devil is in the detail, so make sure you are committing for the right reasons, not out of greed, fear or a sense of duty. The Devil shows some form of toxic environment that you would be better to leave. If you are having a hard time letting go, explore your reasons for this.

REVERSED

The Devil reversed shows that you may have obtained your freedom in some way. Released from a toxic situation, conquered your fears and you are feeling positive. But, those old demons can fight to regain control over you and may resurface. Additional help may be required to maintain your liberty.

MAJOR ARCANA

16.
THE TOWER

Lightening strikes the Tower and leaves the occupants with no other choice than to jump. The Tower represents sudden and unexpected changes in your external circumstances, a disruption in life. But this can be a liberating experience, one you may not immediately feel, but you will have little or no control over it. This is a change that needs to happen even if it feels scary in the moment.

INTERPRETATIONS

UPRIGHT

When the Tower appears in a reading you can expect the unexpected. Something is about to change and it could be a dramatic revelation. If you have been holding onto a defence mechanism and trying to control everything around you, you can be sure of one thing: it is about to change. It is time to adapt to a new way of living and quickly. Embrace the change, it may feel like chaos in the moment, but it will inevitably be for the better.

REVERSED

When reversed, the Tower shows that you may be about to have a narrow escape from something. Fate, the universe, steps in to help you avoid a pitfall. You may find that something shocking occurs, but may have a little more insight prior to the event, lessening the surprise element.

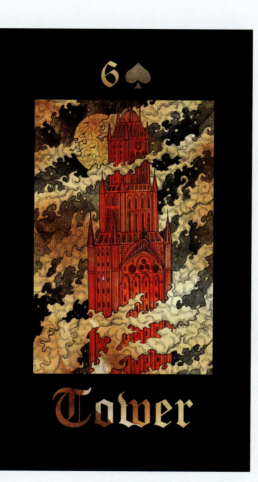

MAJOR ARCANA

17.
THE STAR

he stars have been used for centuries to guide us on both physical and spiritual journeys. The Star represents our inner guidance system and our ability to be in tune with the cosmic energies. It carries the sense of hope and belief in a brighter future. The Star also represents healing, inspiration and assistance from the universe at a time you may need it the most.

INTERPRETATIONS

UPRIGHT

The Star always brings a sense of hope and good fortune to all areas in your life. It is a reminder to not give up on your dreams and to follow your heart. If you are feeling depleted, let the Star's energy heal you through connection with your spiritual side. Keep an optimistic attitude and faith that the universe will help you to achieve your goals. You may have a revelation that helps you to connect with who you truly are.

REVERSED

Even in the reverse, the Star brings its positive healing energy to you. If you are lacking in self belief or motivation right now, then know that miracles can and do happen. Don't be afraid to ask for help. Focus on self-love and healing, and intentionally look for the things that inspire you.

MAJOR ARCANA

18.
THE MOON

The Moon is the most complex of all the cards – it holds mystery and unknown energy. The energy of what is above is below and what is within is without. It shows the distance between the seen and the unseen, and it is a card of confusion and illusion. The Moon shows the darker side of ourselves that is hidden in the shadows, but its reflective light will surely show us what these are. As such, it can leave us feeling unsettled, vulnerable or disorientated.

INTERPRETATIONS

UPRIGHT

When The Moon appears in a reading it is a warning to not trust all that you see or hear. If something feels off, it probably is. However, don't go looking for problems that aren't there. It is a reminder to trust your intuition and to not take everything at face value. You may feel in a state of flux at this time and unclear about what to do next. Wait, as something needs to be revealed before you take action.

REVERSED

The Moon reversed intensifies the state of illusion. You may not be seeing things as they truly are and are refusing to accept the reality of a situation. Being blind to your own, or another's, faults can be destructive. You may discover who or what has been working against you behind the scenes.

The Moon from the 78-card Marseille set.

MAJOR ARCANA

19.
THE SUN

The Sun is positive, full of joy, abundance, youthful exuberance and general good vibes. The child riding the horse represents the inquisitive seeking of joy. It is the card of saying yes to life and love. The Sun illuminates all that is in its path, showing us how we can turn our dreams, as inspired by the Star, into reality. It gives us clarity and truth that the Moon has kept hidden from us. The Sun encourages us to be brave and move on.

INTERPRETATIONS

UPRIGHT

The Sun shows that you are entering a period of joy and optimism. It reminds us that we should have fun and embrace our inner child. Get out and enjoy life and all that it has to offer, say yes to opportunities that come your way. It is time to think positively and expect things to turn out well. You may receive well-deserved rewards at this time. Make time to enjoy the company of friends and family.

REVERSED

Even in the reverse, the Sun still holds positively charged energy. You may find there is a slight delay in experiencing the joy it is bringing, but it is there. Take time to relax if you are exhausted from recent celebrations and don't be too concerned with personal glory at this time.

MAJOR ARCANA

20.
JUDGEMENT

Judgement is not about judging others. It is about finding the truth and making choices that are not concerned with blaming ourselves or others. The three figures in front of Judgement are representations of our past, present and future selves. We have something to liberate of ourselves from the past that will reveal the way we should show up in the present, that will then influence our future path. Judgement is a transformative energy.

INTERPRETATIONS

UPRIGHT

There is a certain amount of realisation that comes when we have Judgement in a reading. You may realise things about yourself or others that need to change. Likewise, you may discover what will never change and this liberates you. Judgement indicates that you are entering a cycle of growth and it is time to leave the past where it belongs, behind you. Look forward, see your true potential and be here now.

REVERSED

You may be refusing to let go of something from your past and it is keeping you stuck in the status quo. You may want everything to remain just as it is, but change is inevitable. You may be forced to move on, even if you don't feel ready, but know that it is for your own good.

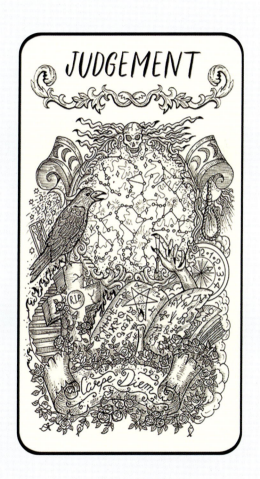

MAJOR ARCANA

21.
THE WORLD

The final card in the major arcana is the World and appropriately, it represents completion. This is a positive card that shows you fulfilling this phase of your life and being ready to move on to the next phase. In the ending is the beginning. The World is about feeling accomplished and being successful. Your hard work is paying off. It may also show the world is your oyster and new destinations are on the horizon.

INTERPRETATIONS

UPRIGHT

The World is cyclical and therefore shows the ending of one cycle and beginning of a new one. In relationships, this can mean moving to the next phase, whether through marriage or being single once again. With work, you may be about to be promoted, change careers or start travelling. The World shows that you are moving toward your goals and success will be yours. Keep focussing on growth as you enter a new phase in life.

REVERSED

You may be having difficulty transitioning into a new life. You may be feeling sad that something is coming to an end and are resisting that change because you don't feel prepared. When the World shows up reversed, it is a reminder to believe in yourself and trust that you are ready.

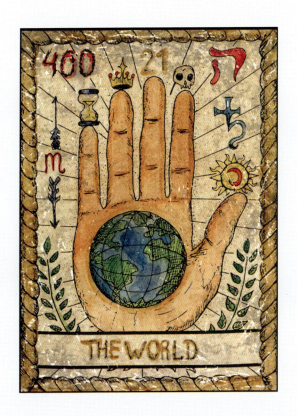

THE MINOR ARCANA

The Minor Arcana, sometimes known as the Lesser Arcana, are the suit cards in a cartomantic tarot deck.

FAR LEFT: Queen of Wands
MIDDLE LEFT: King of Swords
NEAR LEFT: Ace of Cups

MINOR ARCANA

ACE OF CUPS

The Ace of Cups is offering you a gift of divine creative energy. Notice the hand presenting the cup that is overflowing. Cups represent emotions, and the Ace of Cups is the feeling of pure emotion bubbling over with love and inspiration. It is the first card in the suit and as such, represents new love, awareness and connection with your psychic energy.

INTERPRETATIONS

UPRIGHT
When the Ace of Cups is upright in a reading, you can expect magical energy to enter your world. New love or a deepened love of someone is possible when you open your heart. Creativity and imagination will be key to career success, so listen to your heart and your intuition. The Ace of Cups encourages you to find your joy, trust your intuition and listen to your heart for the answers.

REVERSED
If the Ace of Cups is reversed, it's showing the contents have been spilled. You may be feeling disappointed or let down. There may be some unrequited love. Love is lacking in your life in some way. In order to turn it the right way up and refill your cup, look at ways to fill yourself with love again. Self-love, as well as loving others, is key.

MINOR ARCANA

TWO OF CUPS

The Two of Cups represents finding an equal partner, the other half of what you have been missing in your life. You can see the two figures presenting their cups to one another at an equal level, showing that they are sharing their feelings and forming a bond. It is thought of as the Minor Arcana version of the lovers and, as such, it shows the importance of balanced relationships.

INTERPRETATIONS

UPRIGHT
When the Ace of Cups is upright in a reading, you can expect magical When drawn in a love reading, the Two of Cups shows the potential of new love of some kind, or a marriage. It is the alchemical energy of two people merging in an equal way, a balance of power. In a career reading it can show potential partnerships that will be mutually beneficial, or at least a collaboration of some kind. It is important to have your own cup filled so that you come to any situation feeling full of love and confidence

REVERSED
If the Ace of Cups is reversed, it's showing the contents have been If the Two of Cups is reversed then the balance in the relationship may be fractured. You may be giving far more than you are receiving at this time. It can also signify that you have lost your identity as an individual. Remember that you are individuals and you need to stand up in your own right.

MINOR ARCANA

THREE OF CUPS

The Three of Cups represents celebration and joy. You can see three figures raising their cups in triumph and celebrating together. It is the card of friendship and being part of a group. It is about widening your circle from the initial twosome and allowing others to lift your spirits and bring in more joy and happiness, creating your soul tribe who are there for you no matter what.

INTERPRETATIONS

UPRIGHT
When the Three of Cups shows up in a reading it is usually to remind you to have some fun. Life doesn't have to be serious all the time and you don't need to do it alone. You may want to explore making connections with others to enhance your experience in love, work or life in general. Celebrate life, even if you don't feel there is anything to celebrate right now, you'll be amazed how it can lift your spirits.

REVERSED
You may have been partying a little too hard and not spending time focussing on the issues in hand. If so, it is time to sort out your priorities or you will only be left feeling regret or loss. It can also indicate that there may be a third person in a relationship that needs to be looked out for. Don't lose sight of what is important.

MINOR ARCANA

FOUR OF CUPS

In the Four of Cups you can see a figure sitting looking mighty fed up under a tree. He is looking at three empty cups and hasn't noticed, or doesn't want to notice, the cup that is being offered to him. This person appears bored of life, shutting himself off and withdrawing in a negative way. He may feel hurt or rejected or is just simply focussed on all his losses without recognising any of his wins.

INTERPRETATIONS

UPRIGHT
You may be bored in a relationship, or simply unsatisfied. You may feel like you are going through the motions and things are not moving forwards. There could be opportunities in work that you are not seeing the benefit of. Look closely at what you have and appreciate what is right in front of you. But if you want to change something, only you can do that.

REVERSED
It may be time to revisit some past decisions. Maybe you need to say 'yes' to an opportunity that you previously thought was a no-go. Fours indicate a time to stop and be still. As such, it may be time to reflect and check that you are not being overly defensive about something and blocking your own progress.

MINOR ARCANA

FIVE OF CUPS

Fives are never easy cards, the Five of Cups is showing that you may have suffered a loss of something or someone and there is an undeniable sense of disappointment. However, notice the two cups still standing, it may be time to focus on the good in the situation rather than putting all your attention on what you no longer have. Let go of an attachment and don't fear the loss, see it as a chance to begin again.

INTERPRETATIONS

UPRIGHT

You may be wishing you could turn the clock back when you draw the Five of Cups because there is something that you regret. You may feel like the wrong choice has been made and it has lead to a great loss. But look at the figure, he is so focussed on the three spilt cups that he isn't noticing the two still standing, offering new opportunity and insight. Allow yourself to grieve, but don't wallow.

REVERSED

The Five of Cups reversed is a difficult emotion. It is the inability to let go of what has been lost and wallowing in self pity as a result. Try to see the good through the bad and realise that it is all a matter of perspective. Sometimes a loss can lead to a gain. It can also indicate someone coming back into your life with the cups turning back over.

MINOR ARCANA

SIX OF CUPS

The Six of Cups is known as the card of nostalgia. You have two children offering each other flowers. The older child appears to be looking after the younger one. It symbolises a reconnection with someone from your past that you have fond memories of. It is also a reminder to listen to your inner child. It may be time to let your playful side come through without fear, self-doubt and adult inhibitions. It is a sweet card full of innocence.

INTERPRETATIONS

UPRIGHT

People from your past, for bad or good, may show up when you pull this card. If you feel called to reach out to someone, trust your intuition. It's time to put to bed unfinished business and move on. It is the card of nostalgia, so there is usually a good feeling attached to any encounter. You may meet someone you feel you have known for a lifetime. Give out positive vibes, be playful and you will receive good things.

REVERSED

When reversed, the Six of Cups can be the bringer of those things you would rather forget, such as feelings that are keeping you stuck in the past because you just can't let go of them. It is good to look back sometimes, but you don't live there, so let go and move on

MINOR ARCANA

SEVEN OF CUPS

The Seven of Cups shows a figure who is faced with too many options. They have a choice to make, but they are crippled by indecision. This person is finding it difficult to choose because they are stuck trying to see the positive and negative in every situation, making excuses for their indecision. They may also have unrealistic expectations.

INTERPRETATIONS

UPRIGHT

You may be living with an illusion and ignoring the reality of a situation. You could be facing difficult decisions and overthinking, trying to weigh up all the options. Or you may be over-indulging or being lazy. Whichever it is, you need to make a decision. It is time to face your options realistically and commit to your choice.

REVERSED

The confusion of the situation feels too great right now. You may be feeling overwhelmed by the options available to you. This inability to make your mind up or focus could see you missing the opportunity all together. Fear of making the wrong decision is paralysing you. Don't let fear rule your mind, trust your intuition.

MINOR ARCANA

EIGHT OF CUPS

The image in this card shows eight cups neatly yet unevenly stacked, indicating that despite trying to find balance, we cannot. There is something in this situation that is not right, it is not serving us as it should. The figure in the Eight of Cups is walking away from the cups, leaving behind what does not serve them anymore. Although it may leave a heavy feeling in the heart, it is time to change direction.

INTERPRETATIONS

UPRIGHT

Eight of Cups shows up in a reading when it is time to make a change. Change doesn't always feel comfortable and can be scary for some, but it is often necessary and is inevitable. You may feel called to leave a current relationship, or to leave a job or some other situation behind as you explore your options. You may feel sad to say goodbye, but it is important for your personal growth and sense of well-being.

REVERSED

When reversed, the Eight of Cups shows that you may be too afraid to move on and are creating blockages that are keeping you stuck. It can also indicate that someone else is trying to come back into your life who is not ready to release you because they can't move forwards. That is not your problem, it is theirs.

MINOR ARCANA

NINE OF CUPS

The Nine of Cups is known as the wish fulfilled. A feeling of getting all that you want and feeling satisfied. It is a card of wishes being granted and you can see the figure in the picture looks very pleased with himself. He is content, possibly even a little smug about all that he has achieved. A word of caution here – don't alienate others and create envy as this will only bring feelings of resentment and manipulation.

INTERPRETATIONS

UPRIGHT
The Nine of Cups brings pleasure, joy and a feeling of completion to relationships, both personally and professionally. If you are single and looking for love, this may be a sign that someone is about to show up. But don't get complacent if all is going well. You may see everything you have wished for is beginning to show up at this time. This is a time to focus on you and what you want, to indulge in self-love free of guilt.

REVERSED
Reversed may mean there is a delay in receiving what you want or it may not come in the way you were expecting. You could find that great sacrifices have had to be made in order to get what you want, leaving you feeling drained. It also reminds you to not get too full of yourself or you could prevent your wishes from coming true.

MINOR ARCANA

TEN OF CUPS

In the picture on the Ten of Cups, you see the archetypal family looking up at the rainbow filled with cups. This represents fulfilment and all things to be grateful for in life. The ten is a completion of a cycle. You are about to enter a harmonious phase that brings emotional satisfaction and contentment. It is a card filled with positive energy showing that the happiness you seek is within reach.

INTERPRETATIONS

UPRIGHT
When you draw this card in a reading know that positive energy is flowing, so make the most of it. It is a time to find harmony in family and relationships and recognise the positive aspects to be grateful for. This is a card of feeling whole and satisfied in whatever area in your life you are asking about. It is time to receive your heart's desire and appreciate every moment.

REVERSED
If the Ten of Cups is reversed you may be feeling a lack of joy and fulfilment. You want to feel it but something is preventing you. It could be that you are missing something or someone. You may be full of doubt that you can receive all that you desire or are idealising something that you know deep down isn't going to happen.

MINOR ARCANA

PAGE OF CUPS

The Page of Cups brings the youthful energy of love in an idealised and romantic way. He is a dreamer, a creative soul and a romantic at heart. But he is immature, so may be a little naive. He brings you a fish in a cup that indicates a tentative offer of love. It is light-hearted and exciting but may not be a deep, lasting love. The Page of Cups is a sensitive soul, and as such encourages you to be sensitive to both your own and your partner's feelings.

INTERPRETATIONS

UPRIGHT

When the Page of Cups shows up, you could receive an invitation for a date from someone new. This is an opportunity for some light-hearted flirtatious fun. In a career reading, you may be about to get a job offer or be encouraged to follow a more creative path. The Page of Cups is highly sensitive, but still learning, so patience with yourself and others is called for as you develop and grow.

REVERSED

Upright the Page of Cups is so full of optimism, but when he is reversed the opposite is true. It may feel as if all hope is lost. You may be about to experience heartbreak in some way. If you have been a little self-absorbed, it can also be a sign that you need to be more sensitive to others' needs.

MINOR ARCANA

KNIGHT OF CUPS

The Knight of Cups is the proverbial knight in shining armour, rushing in to save his love. He is all about winning hearts with a romantic gesture. However, whether you are the rescuer or the one to be rescued, first establish if this is what is wanted. Knights represent the extremes of the suit, and cups represent emotions. Love isn't all romance and flowers and there may be some petulance and melodrama to deal with too.

INTERPRETATIONS

UPRIGHT
When the Ace of Cups is upright in a reading, you can expect magical The Knight of Cups is the dreamer, the romantic and when he shows up in a reading, he can bring great joy and expectation. As he's a messenger, you may be about to hear from someone offering you a date or even a proposal. You are encouraged to follow your heart, trust your intuition and believe in your dreams at this time. Anything is possible!

REVERSED
As with the Page of Cups, when reversed, the Knight of Cups can symbolise heartbreak or disappointment. You may need to ask yourself: are you in love with the person or the idea of being in love? It is time to take a good look at what is genuine and see if you need a reality check.

MINOR ARCANA

QUEEN OF CUPS

The Queen of Cups is the most caring and compassionate of all the queens in the deck. She is emotionally aware, tender-hearted and highly intuitive. There is no hiding your true feelings from the Queen of Cups – she will know if you are putting on a brave face. Your priority is one of deep emotional empathy when she shows up in a reading. You are loved unconditionally and patience is a virtue to appreciate.

INTERPRETATIONS

UPRIGHT

When the Queen of Cups appears in a reading, trust your instincts and you will not go wrong. It is time to be heart-led and open to exploring your emotions. Either you or someone you are interacting with will display a good deal of patience and understanding and this is needed here. She is a healer, so you may need to nurture yourself or someone else. Psychic abilities are heightened with her presence, so trust your intuition.

REVERSED

When reversed, the Queen of Cups may show that there is some emotional manipulation going on, either from you or someone in your life. Try to look at yourself objectively. Are you being needy, suffering from low self-worth? Are you repressing your own emotional needs?

MINOR ARCANA

KING OF CUPS

The King of Cups is a calm, stable, wise and diplomatic king. He displays an emotional maturity that may be lacking elsewhere. He is intuitive like his counterpart, the Queen, but kindness and compassion are his main traits. The King of Cups nurtures and cares for you and is someone that you can always count on to be there when needed. His energy says that there is a need for a calm approach in times chaos.

INTERPRETATIONS

UPRIGHT

The King of Cups in a reading always indicates the need to be more heart-led, to open up your feelings and use your intuition to guide you. You may need to be patient with yourself, others or a situation. Learn to weigh up the pros and cons and don't rush in. If this king represents someone in your life, they are a patient and kind soul who is easy to talk to and get advice from without judgement.

REVERSED

The King of Cups reversed lacks the emotional maturity of the upright king. He may be petulant and manipulative and is looking for ways to escape the realities of life. If this is you, then you may need to explore your emotions to discover the truth about what you want. If it is another person, then you may find they are exercising control over you.

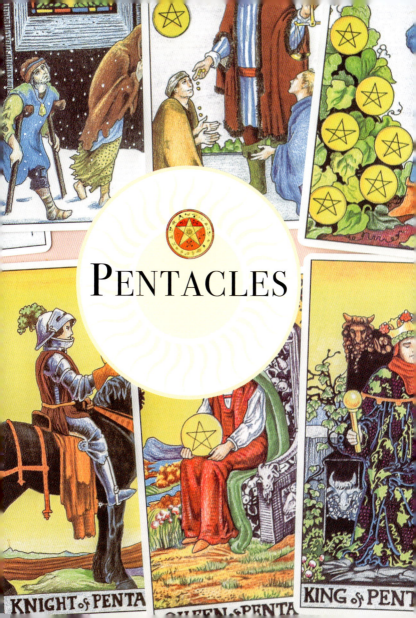

Pentacles

MINOR ARCANA

ACE OF PENTACLES

The hand that offers the pentacle is cupped to keep it safe. It represents a seed that is ready to be planted. This ace is the sign that you are ready to invest your time, energy and resources into building something tangible. This is not something insignificant, this is a foundation to support a better future. It is time to sow the seeds of success, so look for real and measurable opportunities.

INTERPRETATIONS

UPRIGHT
The Ace of Pentacles represents solid foundations in whatever area of your life you are querying – a new and stable beginning that will reap long-term rewards. It is time to invest in your future in a very tangible way. This may take time, effort and energy, but the pay-off will be worth it. You can look forward to the resources you need becoming available.

REVERSED
The Ace of Pentacles reversed could indicate an investment that has gone, or is about to go, wrong. A contract or commitment may be broken. Or it could just be a change of heart. You need to decide if it is worth salvaging, or if it is time to cut your losses and walk away. It can also show an unhealthy attachment to material gains to the detriment of spiritual needs.

MINOR ARCANA

TWO OF PENTACLES

The Two of Pentacles depicts a person juggling and that sums up what this card means. Life can be a juggling act, the key is to have fun with it and enjoy the dance. There are infinite possibilities and sometimes we need to play with our energy and go with the flow. However, at some point you may need help to regain your balance so that you don't drop the ball or, in this instance, the pentacle.

INTERPRETATIONS

UPRIGHT

The Ace of Pentacles represents solid foundations in whatever area of your If the Two of Pentacles shows up in a reading, then you are either feeling a bit overwhelmed by all the responsibilities you have to deal with, or at least need to redress the balance. In love, it may indicate a need to explore your options. You need to have a little more confidence in your abilities when this card shows up and learn to adapt to changes.

REVERSED

The proverbial balls have been dropped when the Two of Pentacles is reversed. You may have taken on too much and it is proving impossible to keep everything working together. It is time to slow down and maybe to ask for some help to get you back on track. Re-group and think how you can develop a better plan.

MINOR ARCANA

THREE OF PENTACLES

The key elements of the Three of Pentacles are cooperation and collaboration. With support, planning and teamwork a successful project can be achieved. In this card you see the two religious figures supporting the artist while he works on creating a statue, looking on without interference. Sometimes all we need is to feel valued and have our hard work recognised.

INTERPRETATIONS

UPRIGHT

In the upright position, the Three of Pentacles shows that you may be beginning to feel recognised for all your endeavours. Whether personally or professionally, you feel noticed and appreciated. It may take some cooperation and equal effort between you and others to succeed. Alternatively you may be wanting to stand out from the crowd and not be just another cog in the wheel. This is a time of great personal growth.

REVERSED

When reversed, you may be spending too much time seeking other people's approval. You should be prepared to be more independent and not be reliant on what others think. Or you may be hyper-focussed on the details and not be able to see the bigger picture. Whatever happens, you may not be able to rely on others for support right now.

MINOR ARCANA

FOUR OF PENTACLES

The figure in the Four of Pentacles is quite obviously holding onto what he has. He has worked hard for his money and achievements and he is reluctant to let it go. This person can be seen a miserly or mean, being possessive about what he owns. However, it can be that he is finally feeling a sense of stability, or wanting to save for the future. It is the card of banking what you have and not wanting to let go it.

INTERPRETATIONS

UPRIGHT

The Four of Pentacles in a reading indicates some form of stubbornness, usually for good. You may need to take control of a situation and plan more conservatively. You may be putting your money away and investing wisely for your future. It is okay if you need to be a little more selfish with your time and emotions, you may need time to heal.

REVERSED

When reversed, the Four of Pentacles can indicate that someone is being unkind or miserly in your life – maybe you! Whatever the situation, a healthy resilient attitude is bordering on stinginess at this time. Think about ways to be more flexible and open. Remember, sometimes we need to spend money to make money.

MINOR ARCANA

FIVE OF PENTACLES

In this card you can see there are two poor figures out in the snow, dressed in rags. There is a window with the five pentacles behind them, but they don't seem to notice it. This pretty much depicts the feeling of the card. There is a sense of loss but, more than that, there's also a feeling of being abandoned, left out in the cold and feeling something is missing. However, is this self-inflicted or has something been done to them?

INTERPRETATIONS

UPRIGHT
The Five of Pentacles always conveys a sense that something is lacking in your life. Whether spiritually, emotionally or physically, there is something that you need and don't yet have. If you are feeling abandoned by people, or circumstances have left you feeling less than whole, take heart that this card shows that it is time to go and discover what is missing. Some self-care is called for here, so look out for yourself first.

REVERSED
When reversed, the Five of Pentacles shows that you may have hit rock bottom emotionally, feeling lonely, isolated and hopeless. You may feel you have asked for help and it has been ignored. But rather than wallow in victimhood, it is time to rescue yourself and take back control of your own destiny.

MINOR ARCANA

SIX OF PENTACLES

The Six of Pentacles is known as the card of 'the gift'. You can see the person with wealth giving to one of the beggars, while holding the scales of justice in the other hand. This shows that there are some people who get and some who do not but, more than that, someone makes those choices. It is a card of give and take, so the importance of the scales is also one of balance, a balance of power and wealth, as well as giving and receiving.

INTERPRETATIONS

UPRIGHT

You may be about to receive a gift of money in some way when this card shows up in your reading. But equally it can be that you are in need of giving as much as you are taking, especially in matters of the heart. There may be an imbalance that needs to be addressed. However, don't be afraid to ask for what you need in life at this time, you may be pleasantly surprised by what you are given.

REVERSED

You may be about to receive a gift of money in some way when this card shows up in your reading. But equally it can be that you are in need of giving as much as you are taking, especially in matters of the heart. There may be an imbalance that needs to be addressed. However, don't be afraid to ask for what you need in life at this time, you may be pleasantly surprised by what you are given.

MINOR ARCANA

SEVEN OF PENTACLES

You can see the gardener surveying his efforts in the Seven of Pentacles, showing that he has come to a place where he could reap the rewards, harvest his crop. However, this brings up some issues of 'what next?' and fear of moving on. It is time to assess and evaluate your efforts so far, looking at how far you have come and taking a step back to think about where you are heading.

INTERPRETATIONS

UPRIGHT

In a reading, the Seven of Pentacles encourages you to take stock of what you have achieved and how far you have come, and to realistically evaluate a situation and possibly take a break. It may be time to move onto something new. Take a step back and look at the bigger picture. What is going to help you to move forwards and what is your next goal?

REVERSED

Now is not the time to sit around and do nothing, you have come so far, now you need to act. Maybe you have not achieved what you thought you would have by now, it could be time to try a different approach or walk away altogether. More effort in the same endeavour will not give you what you need, so it's time to try something different.

MINOR ARCANA

EIGHT OF PENTACLES

The Eight of Pentacles shows a man with a chisel in his hand knocking out the pentacles. The work ahead may be repetitive, mundane or even boring, but it is necessary. Now is the time to focus your energy on the task in hand, whether it is with work, love or self. Show those who have invested in you what you are made of. It is time to prove your worth and feel confident in your ability to do so.

INTERPRETATIONS

UPRIGHT

Your investment in getting the job done and the quality of your work will speak for themselves. You are doing all you can to build healthy relationships, move forwards in your career or discover your purpose in life. The Eight of Pentacles in the upright is encouragement to keep going – a job well done will reap its own rewards.

REVERSED

When reversed, the Eight of Pentacles may indicate that you have been focussing too much on material gain at the expense of loved ones and personal relationships. It may also show that you, or someone close to you, is not committed to putting in real work and is instead looking for shortcuts. You may be struggling with motivation and focus.

MINOR ARCANA

NINE OF PENTACLES

The Nine of Pentacles shows a woman in her garden surveying all that she has accomplished. The hooded falcon on her hand shows the level of control she now has – it has been trained and has come back to her. To an outsider, this may look like you have all that you need and want, but let's not forget the effort and work it took to get here. This is a well-deserved, well-earned time of reward, reaping what you have sown.

INTERPRETATIONS

UPRIGHT
You are entering into a time of reward and gratification when the Nine of Pentacles shows up in a reading. Your hard work is paying off and is giving you a sense of independence and self-sufficiency. It may be that you are realising that you are in control of your own life and you don't need anyone else to make you happy. Focus on self-love and well-being.

REVERSED
When the Nine of Pentacles shows up reversed, it may be that you have achieved financial success, but at what cost? Money cannot buy happiness or love. Have you been too focussed on achieving material wealth at the expense of personal growth? You may be feeling a low sense of self-worth, which has caused you to focus too much on money.

MINOR ARCANA

TEN OF PENTACLES

The Ten of Pentacles depicts perfect family, wealth and friends – the good life. But do you want to follow convention? This card does show wealth is often linked with a familial connection, such as a trust fund or inheritance. It can also depict a past or long-term investment finally coming to fruition. Generally speaking, it shows a phase of prosperity that is closely linked with your roots.

INTERPRETATIONS

UPRIGHT
This card usually shows that financial security, family and a good community are at your disposal. It is a positive card, but remember, there is no harm in wanting something more. This is a time to examine how you can create long-term stability, emotionally and financially. Family is important, but you need to assess whether you are doing this for you or because of family expectations.

REVERSED
life, your wealth and your security is crumbling around you. The focus may be on creating financial stability in the belief that this will fix all your problems, but you need to look deeper into this. You may be struggling to move forwards because fear of failure is holding you back.

MINOR ARCANA

PAGE OF PENTACLES

The Page of Pentacles represents a practical approach to your future. He appears when you are needing to set realistic goals and indicates that planning and slow, steady progress are the way forward. Think of it as setting the wheels in motion for the next phase of your life, while recognising all you have achieved to date. This is an opportunity to progress, but you need to look for it and be prepared to take action. Patience and diligence are key to this Page's energy.

INTERPRETATIONS

UPRIGHT

As the Page of Pentacles is a messenger with earth energy, you may receive news about work or financial opportunities. His presence indicates that now is the time to commit to creating those solid foundations upon which to build a future, whether personally or professionally. This card shows that this is a time to be patient with yourself, you still have a lot to learn.

REVERSED

When the Page of Pentacles is reversed, it can often indicate that someone is reluctant to put in the effort required to be successful. They lack commitment and adopt an attitude of putting things off. You may be looking for the easy way, or, alternatively have become so hyper-focussed on the details that you become stuck. It may be time to let go.

MINOR ARCANA

KNIGHT OF PENTACLES

The Knight of Pentacles is Mr Plod, he is about slow, steady progress. Although he is willing to put in the effort and work hard towards achieving his goal, this can be with a complete lack of passion or excitement. This knight does show that you are closer to achieving what you set out to do and that your hard work is starting to pay off. But he does carry a warning of being unadventurous in your endeavours.

INTERPRETATIONS

UPRIGHT

The Knight of Pentacles in a reading indicates consistent effort with emotional detachment. That may work for a project that needs completing but is not so great for a relationship. Although this knight is trustworthy and loyal, he is not the most exciting. He is a good omen for work and career as he shows that your dedication will pay off. He thrives in routine and demonstrates a need to be mindful of not missing any steps.

REVERSED

Reversed, this knight can signify a certain level of pessimism, feeling detached from what you are doing. You may be feeling insecure and unstable. If he relates to a relationship, it may show that the person you are with is no longer willing to put in the effort, leaving you feeling uncertain about your future together.

MINOR ARCANA

QUEEN OF PENTACLES

The Queen of Pentacles is a real earth mother figure. She is stable, practical, sensual and sensitive to the needs of others. She has reached a point in her life where she is secure emotionally, and is reliable and nurturing. This queen is connected deeply with family and always makes time for them and close friends. This is the feminine energy of nurture and being down to earth, regardless of the gender of the enquirer.

INTERPRETATIONS

UPRIGHT
When the Queen of Pentacles shows up in a reading, she either represents someone in your life who is very nurturing, kind and practical, or a need for you to find those qualities in yourself. It may be time to show yourself the love you deserve. It's time to work on your dreams and allow the steady hand of this queen to guide you. She represents growth and fertility – all that you touch at this time could turn to gold.

REVERSED
When reversed you may be detached from reality, finding it hard to focus and make decisions. You may no longer be working on your dreams because it just all seems like too much effort. Instead you may be looking for someone else to do the work. Alternatively, you could be so focussed on looking after everyone else's needs that you are neglecting your own.

MINOR ARCANA

KING OF PENTACLES

This King has made it. He is at the top of his game, financially set, stable, secure, reliable and dependable. Like his counterpart, the King of Pentacles is gentle and kind, and a family man. He will do what he needs to do to grow and be successful in a dedicated and compassionate way. This is a king who is happy and content and he is the sort of person you want in your life.

INTERPRETATIONS

UPRIGHT

in your life. So enjoy it and don't feel guilty, your hard work is really about to pay off. He may be someone who could help you and guide you to financial success. In love, if this king is committing to you, you can be sure he is all in and will want to care for you. This card shows patience and feeling worthy are the cornerstones to happiness.

REVERSED

Reversed, this king can be stubborn and stingy, focussing too much on material gain to the detriment of his relationships. Rather than being kind and considerate, he shows a disregard for others' feelings and may be a bit self-indulgent. It could be someone else who is expecting you to take on too much.

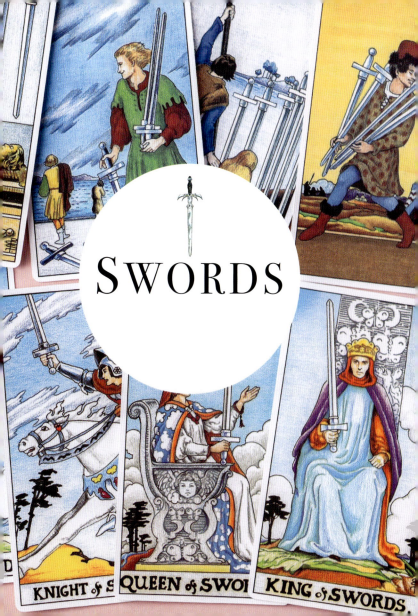

MINOR ARCANA

ACE OF SWORDS

The Ace of Swords shows a double-edged sword being handed through the clouds. The sword can be used for both protection and destruction. It can signify great clarity, clear thinking and using your intellect wisely. But it can also show challenges ahead and a need to be honest with yourself. Sword energy removes emotion from the equation and encourages clear thinking.

INTERPRETATIONS

UPRIGHT

In a reading, the Ace of Swords shows that logic over feelings or intuition is ruling right now. You may find that you hear things you don't want to in a relationship. However, in a career reading it shows that you are ready to use your rational head and have the clear-thinking ability to accomplish whatever you want. The power of this card lays in its ability to manifest your desires with the power of focus.

REVERSED

The reversed energy of this card can be very destructive. You may be over analysing a situation without really getting to the heart of the matter. Or you could be experiencing pain or upsetting others because feelings are being disregarded. Now is not the time to intentionally abuse others. Remember that this sword has two edges and the likelihood is that what you put out is what you get back.

MINOR ARCANA

TWO OF SWORDS

The figure here sits with a blindfold on and the two swords are crossed. The implication is that you are at a crossroads and can't, or don't, want to see which direction to go in. The swords are also crossed over the heart showing that you are feeling the need to protect yourself, however nothing can come in or get out, so there is a lack of self-expression here too. You may feel defensive, which is making you indecisive.

INTERPRETATIONS

UPRIGHT

You may need to take time to figure out what you want, and feel your feelings. Are you blocking something out because of fear or because it is uncomfortable? Are you being blind to the truth in a situation? Whatever is going on, the energy is stuck at this time. Sometimes all we can do is wait until the dust settles so that we can see more clearly the direction that we should be going in.

REVERSED

Reversed, the Two of Swords can indicate that you have been stuck for so long that you have totally shut down emotionally. It may be time for you to let down the barrier and be open to seeing or hearing the truth. You may have been reluctant to take time for yourself and this is clouding your judgement. The good thing is, this energy may be about to shift. .

MINOR ARCANA

THREE OF SWORDS

The Three of Swords is known as the card of heartbreak. You can see the three swords piercing the heart, illustrating your hurt and disappointment. Maybe there is a third person in your relationship, a betrayal of the heart. You may be able to finally get to the heart of the matter and work out what to do, if you can be honest with yourself. There are a lot of feelings of loss, hurt, injustice and rejection, so if you need to cry then do, don't hold onto negative emotions.

INTERPRETATIONS

UPRIGHT
When the Three of Swords shows up in a reading, you are about to have, or have just had, some kind of emotional trauma. Although you may have good reason to feel disappointed, you may also be over-dramatising the situation. The good thing about this card is that you can use it to assess what is really going on and start to heal your wounds. Open your heart and feel.

REVERSED
Sometimes the pain is so deep it becomes all-consuming and that is the energy that the Three of Swords in reverse brings. Take an honest look at what is going on: are you making yourself feel worse by focussing solely on that heartache? Can you refocus your energy into healing?

MINOR ARCANA

FOUR OF SWORDS

The Four of Swords shows a figure in a state of suspended animation, in rest. This is the time for taking a step back and finding your sense of equilibrium. Take stock of a situation and explore the innermost fears that could be holding you back. The rest could be as simple as taking a nap or meditating, or perhaps taking a short holiday.

INTERPRETATIONS

UPRIGHT
What fears are holding you back? Are you full of self-doubt? Are things not going the way you had planned? These are important questions to ask yourself when the Four of Swords appears in a reading. Answer with a rested mind and you will find the answers. Think of it as preparing for what is to come. Do you need a sabbatical from life, love or work? Whatever is going on, taking a break is essential to figuring out your next move.

REVERSED
The number four is associated with stubbornness, but a refusal to take a break could lead to burnout. You may be in a frozen wasteland of unresolved feelings and there will be a need to explore those with a clear and constructive attitude. Alternatively, you may find that you are coming out of a period of rest feeling refreshed and ready to start again.

MINOR ARCANA

FIVE OF SWORDS

The Five of Swords shows two figures walking away in defeat while the one at the front is claiming victory. This dual energy is prevalent in so far as, which one are you? Do you want to win at all costs, even if it is to the detriment of others? This can be a destructive energy with people exacting revenge and making pointless power plays. It can equally show that you have conquered your fears and won against the odds.

INTERPRETATIONS

UPRIGHT
Be warned that in a relationship, this shows that there is a big ego at play and compromise is not in their vocabulary. In working relationships there may be someone who is working against you causing friction and unnecessary tension. Be aware of hollow victories at this time and be honest with yourself about your own actions. The truth will set you free and help you to grow.

REVERSED
When the Five of Swords is reversed, you really need to be on the lookout for people who are playing power games, using others to further their own lives and totally disregarding their feelings. You may be being bullied or are bullying someone else. This energy is one of attack and aggression and you need to be on your guard.

MINOR ARCANA

SIX OF SWORDS

Finally we can start to see the troubles being left behind with the Six of Swords. The image shows a boat loaded up with all that is remaining of you and the figure is pushing the boat out of troubled choppy waters towards calmer ones. It is time for recovery, it is time to leave the past behind and begin the journey towards a more positive outlook on life. This card brings the chance for a new perspective.

INTERPRETATIONS

UPRIGHT
It is time to move forwards when the Six of Swords appears in a reading. You may feel exhausted mentally and physically, but help is there to aid you with leaving the destructive past behind. It is time for the next phase in your journey. Think of it as leaving your worries behind and embracing the next phase of your life. Co-operation and mutual awareness will help you to solve your issues.

REVERSED
When the Six of Swords shows up reversed, you haven't left your troubles behind, something is still lingering. Stop worrying about the what-ifs of the situation because these are keeping you from moving on. You need to let go of the emotional baggage and use your sense of logic to confront the real issue in hand.

MINOR ARCANA

SEVEN OF SWORDS

You can see the person in this card looking very shifty indeed. He is sneaking off with the swords, sure he will get away with it, stealing what is not his. That is basically the energy of this card – sneaky underhanded behaviour, cheating and lying. Not facing the truth but using deception to avoid taking responsibility. This is a scary card to get, but don't run away from the truth, rather seek it out at this time.

INTERPRETATIONS

UPRIGHT
The Seven of Swords in a reading asks you to be honest and face the truth in any given situation. You may be deceiving yourself, convinced that what you are doing is the right thing, but you know deep down it isn't. Or it could be that you need to watch your back. Someone is trying to deceive you or place the blame on you for their mistake.

REVERSED
Are you making things worse for yourself by not being honest? Be warned, when the Seven of Swords is in the reverse, that truth will out. If it is someone who has been working against you behind the scenes, you may finally find out who that is. This could lead to you getting back what was taken from you or at least receiving an apology.

MINOR ARCANA

EIGHT OF SWORDS

You will see that there is a woman bound and blindfolded in this card, surrounded by swords. This shows that you may be feeling trapped and bound by a situation that you can't see a way out of. However, she could, if she wanted to, free herself from those binds. It takes using the sword energy here – focus and clarity – to see the situation as it truly is.

INTERPRETATIONS

UPRIGHT

You may be feeling trapped, expecting the worst to happen when the Eight of Swords shows up in a reading. Your fear of what might happen is controlling your waking thoughts. Trust may have been lost and you fear you won't get it back. There is a need to protect yourself and you may even be looking to be rescued. However, it is your inner strength and the ability to think logically and rationally that will help you escape.

REVERSED

There are two possible emotions behind this card reversed. You may feel even more trapped, slipping into depression, finding it impossible to wriggle out of those binds. Or, you may be starting to peak out from behind the blindfold and see things for what they really are – a realisation that your own fear is all that is holding you back.

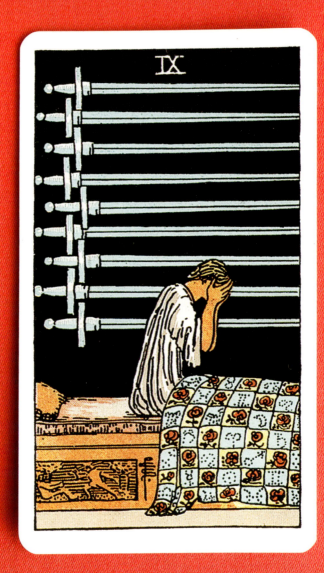

MINOR ARCANA

NINE OF SWORDS

The figure on the Nine of Swords card is seen sitting up in bed with his head in his hands, showing the sleepless nights he is suffering. This is a card of stress and worry that at times can feel overwhelming. There is a lot of self doubt, guilt and regret associated with this card. It is possibly the most difficult card to receive in tarot. Everyone has suffered a stressful night of tossing and turning but remember that it is always darkest before the dawn.

INTERPRETATIONS

UPRIGHT

Whatever your question, when you draw the Nine of Swords, you are worried about something, suffering and stressing. You need to work out what is making you feel this way. You may be finding it difficult to express how you truly feel, or feeling totally alone and isolated. You may be looking for some emotional support, or feeling guilt or shame for something. It is time to refocus on what it is you truly want.

REVERSED

When this card is reversed you really are in a state of heightened anxiety and stress. Your sleepless nights are preventing you from thinking clearly and you are stuck in a loop of self doubt and worry. You need help to guide you out of the darkness. Alternatively, you may be finally seeing the way forward.

MINOR ARCANA

TEN OF SWORDS

As scary as this card looks, it is a ten, which means that you are reaching the end of a cycle. When you hit rock bottom the only way is up. It is time to liberate yourself from your emotional baggage and face up to what you need to let go of. It is time to find your sense of enlightenment with a new self-awareness that comes from examining your behaviour patterns and motives.

INTERPRETATIONS

UPRIGHT

Know that whatever you are going through is coming to an end when the Ten of Swords shows up in a reading. It is time to let go of past hurts and either leave a relationship or work through those issues. You may have lost a job or be changing career when this card appears but either way there is a cycle that is coming to its end. Now is the time to look forwards and let go of negative thinking.

REVERSED

Are you playing the victim or the martyr? The Ten of Swords reversed shows that you may be holding onto something that you really need to release. You may feel sad to say goodbye to your old life, feel disappointed, but the only way forwards is to cut those ties. Alternatively, the swords have been removed and now is the time to heal. There is always a reason – have you learned your lesson?

MINOR ARCANA

PAGE OF SWORDS

The Page of Swords, as with all pages, is a messenger. He is bringing you news that will be the truth, whether you want to hear it or not. The youthful energy of this page brings a sense of honesty that is refreshing, even if it is challenging. He is ready for action and wants to convey his knowledge and wisdom with you. This page brings intellect and logic but doesn't always consider your feelings.

INTERPRETATIONS

UPRIGHT

You can expect some sort of challenge when the Page of Swords appears in a reading. Use your own sense of logic and circumspection to help you navigate the situation and try to remain detached from the emotional side. You may be hearing about a work opportunity, but the page doesn't guarantee a favourable outcome. Be prepared to learn, research and communicate with clarity.

REVERSED

You may not receive the news you were expecting as it could be blocked in some way. This news isn't necessarily bad, with the Page of Swords it can go either way. But be aware of what you are saying at this time, don't pretend to know all the answers. Others may find your words harsh at this time and they could potentially come back to bite you.

MINOR ARCANA

KNIGHT OF SWORDS

The Knight of Swords comes charging in like a hurricane. His energy is fast and furious, and full of force. This can leave you feeling a little knocked off balance if you are not ready for it. He is a very self-assured knight, and can be impetuous and a little brusque. He is intellectual and you may find yourself having very spirited conversations with highly intelligent people when he rushes in.

INTERPRETATIONS

UPRIGHT
If you receive the Knight of Swords in a reading be prepared to engage your brain. Don't rush into situations without carefully strategising first. If you do things in haste, you will repent at leisure, as they say. Think through the consequences and you will do well. Be ready for action, but do your research and make sure you are fully informed before moving. A bold, confident approach is needed.

REVERSED
In the reverse, the Knight of Swords may represent someone who is being overbearing and not allowing you to express your needs. They can be brutally honest without consideration of feelings. It can be someone who is deliberately being antagonistic to provoke you or even to sabotage your efforts. Make sure it is not you who is being cruel.

MINOR ARCANA

QUEEN OF SWORDS

I like to think of the Queen of Swords as the warrior queen. She is tough, independent, astute, honest, direct and quick-witted. She is a highly intelligent individual with a no-nonsense approach to life. This queen has earned her throne through hard work and her ability to resolve problems quickly and efficiently. However, all this tough exterior has left her a little detached from her emotions, so her honesty can sometimes sting.

INTERPRETATIONS

UPRIGHT
Love may take a back seat in your life if you draw the Queen of Swords in a reading. Your focus may be more on intellectual pursuits or career. If work is your primary focus then the queen is a positive influence. Her dedication to research, rational thinking and her honesty are positives. Being able to separate emotions from decision-making can help you make good judgement calls.

REVERSED
This is not a queen you want to come into contact with when she is reversed. She is so detached from her emotions that she seems to derive pleasure from making others suffer. There is a complete lack of consideration and she is manipulative and intimidating to be around.

MINOR ARCANA

KING OF SWORDS

The King of Swords is very self-assured. He is highly intelligent, logical and a true leader. This is the king you would follow into battle. He doesn't have time for idle chit-chat and so when he does speak, it is articulate and to the point. He has high standards and will use his logical objectivity to make fair judgements. This king does not show his emotions – he is far too analytical for that. But he can appear inflexible as he always follows the rules.

INTERPRETATIONS

UPRIGHT

This king is all about intellect so he is not the best person to be in a relationship with as he will never share his feelings with you – he is happier alone. But in a work situation, he can represent someone who will challenge you to improve. You are encouraged to use your intellect, do your research, show your determination and be motivated to succeed when the King of Swords appears in a reading.

REVERSED

The King of Swords reversed can be terrifying. If it is you, consider if you are blocking out your feelings so much that you are being too assertive. The energy of this king reversed is manipulative, cruel and intimidating. He wants to dominate and doesn't stop to consider anyone's feelings.

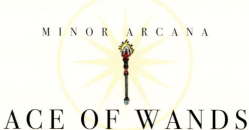

MINOR ARCANA

ACE OF WANDS

As with all aces, the Ace of Wands signifies that something new is beginning. It brings a new adventure, a new lease of life, with a sense of excitement and awe. The wand is being handed to you with fresh new leaves, symbolising the possibility for growth. It is time to be fearless and take action towards achieving your goals. You may feel inspired, with creative juices flowing, but you need to act on this to set things in motion.

INTERPRETATIONS

UPRIGHT

When the Ace of Wands appears in a reading you may find that you start to feel inspired and you believe in your ability to carry out your plans. It signifies a new beginning, a fresh start wrapped up in excitement and passion for what you are about to do. Delve into the things that excite you and ignite your sense of adventure. Be warned though, a new love affair may be all passion and no substance.

REVERSED

When reversed, you may be being a bit too pushy, a bit too sure of yourself, so know your limitations. Or you may find that the spark of enthusiasm has extinguished. You are finding it hard to feel passionate about anything. You may have been let down and now feel hopeless.

MINOR ARCANA

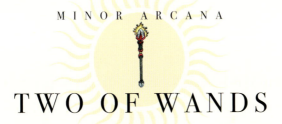

TWO OF WANDS

I love the Two of Wands, which is all about potential. You can see the figure in the card holding a globe in his hand and a wand in the other, literally feeling like he has the whole world in his hands. Likewise though, one wand is standing neglected, showing the split energy of this card. The question is, are you excited to see what the world has to offer or are you going to stick with what you know just because it is familiar?

INTERPRETATIONS

UPRIGHT

When the Two of Wands is in the upright, you may feel your sense of power and prowess growing, ready to embrace new challenges and ideas. It is a good time to think about collaborating with others to supercharge your success. You may even be looking at international connections. Embrace the excitement of potential and be ready to seize opportunities when they arise.

REVERSED

Your sense of enthusiasm may not be reciprocated by others and you start to feel the potential slipping away when the Two of Wands is reversed. Others may have a different agenda and be trying to bend you to their will. Networking and making connections is difficult at this time. You may even have a trip cancelled for some reason.

MINOR ARCANA

THREE OF WANDS

You can see the figure in the card staring out across the landscape contemplating where he is going next. He is waiting for his ships to come in after all the planning and collaborating on his ideas. The Three of Wands brings a sense of adventure and a willingness to explore the possibilities that are opening up in front of him. This comes with careful planning and foresight, not just blindly jumping into something without thinking it through.

INTERPRETATIONS

UPRIGHT

When you draw this card in the upright position, it is time to start putting your plans into action and to show others what you are capable of. There is still an element of waiting involved but there is also evidence of growth. You are looking towards the future, which isn't here yet but feels optimistic. Foresight is your gift, so be prepared for obstacles.

REVERSED

Are you too focussed on where you want to be without recognising where you are now? This can lead to frustration and your impatience may block your progress. Others may not do what they said they would. That initial excitement could be dwindling when the Three of Wands is reversed and you may be considering alternatives.

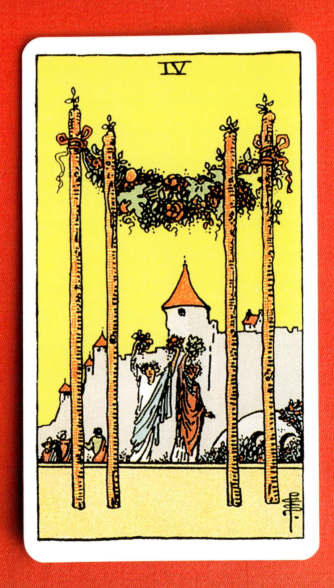

MINOR ARCANA

FOUR OF WANDS

The Four of Wands is the card of celebration and jubilation. You can see the figures in the card filled with joy and happiness. They are dancing towards a happy life, feeling free and exuberant. This card is a true blessing, it shows that they are on the path to success and they should feel proud of all their achievements. It also shows a level of support with solid foundations that the number four provides. This is a lucky period.

INTERPRETATIONS

UPRIGHT
There is a sense of freedom that comes with the Four of Wands, so if you have been feeling stuck, expect opportunities to break free. This is time to celebrate. In a relationship, it can indicate a marriage or some other celebration of a milestone. In work you can expect success, all that you touch turning to gold. Life feels good at this time.

REVERSED
There is still the chance that you may be able to set your foundations to build the future you want when the Four of Wands is reversed. But there may be some delays. If you are afraid of moving on or making changes, you may be blocking the joyous feeling. You may not have the 'perfect' celebration but remember, every win is worth celebrating.

MINOR ARCANA

FIVE OF WANDS

Fives are never easy, but the Five of Wands may be used to your advantage. You can see the figures fighting, competing with one another. This shows that some sort of struggle is taking place and there is no clear winner at this point. But this could be a chance for one person to prove their worth, to step up and show the others what they are made of. At this moment the competition looks pretty even, so how can you stand out?

INTERPRETATIONS

UPRIGHT
There is some form of competition or rivalry when the Five of Wands shows up in a reading. Just be sure to pick your battles and don't get into petty arguments just to prove a point. However, if you are competing for a promotion or to win a contract, now is the time to step up and shine. Be assertive, but be mindful of your motives. It is okay to rise to a challenge when it is for the right reasons.

REVERSED
Are you trying to use others to put yourself ahead? Be sure that this will inevitably backfire when the Five of Wands shows up reversed. You may find that the competition is a lot stronger than you had anticipated. Are you willing to step up your efforts? Or is this bringing up feelings of insecurity that will make you retreat?

MINOR ARCANA

SIX OF WANDS

The Six of Wands is the card of success and triumph. You can see the figure on horseback enjoying his victory parade. People are cheering him on and celebrating his success. He is well and truly in the spotlight and loving it. He has won, and he is enjoying the accolades. The only caution with this card is to not get on your high horse and feel superior to others because of all you have achieved.

INTERPRETATIONS

UPRIGHT

When you draw this card then you may be feeling on top of the world, like you can achieve anything. But remember that pride comes before a fall, so enjoy the attention but know that success is something to be shared, not used to lord over others. You can expect to get the job, person or results you want. Focus on what you want and recognise both your strengths and weaknesses.

REVERSED

You may be feeling unappreciated if the Six of Wands shows up reversed in a reading. The promotion you went for could have gone to someone else. You may have been expecting too much, or relying too much on other people's opinions. Whatever is happening, the success you are experiencing is not living up to expectations.

MINOR ARCANA

SEVEN OF WANDS

The Seven of Wands is all about defiant behaviour, standing up for yourself and believing in yourself. You can see the figure in a defensive stance ready to do battle. This is not a passive card, rather one of fighting for your rights. Whatever the opposition, he is ready to defend his stance and is refusing to budge. It may be a pointless battle, but this figure is ready to say no and is resolute in his convictions.

INTERPRETATIONS

UPRIGHT

This is the card of determination. When it shows upright, you are willing to, and probably have to, fight for what you want, whether that is for a person, a job or some recognition. Now is the time to say 'no', set your boundaries and don't compromise on what you want. You may come up against opposition, but have the courage of your convictions. Speak your truth and be willing to share your creative insights.

REVERSED

When reversed, the Seven of Wands shows that you may be struggling to make a stand, being a people-pleaser and not wanting to rock the boat. Your confidence is wavering and you are not sure that you have what it takes to go into battle. You may feel like giving up and backing down. You may not win, but ask yourself, is it worth trying?

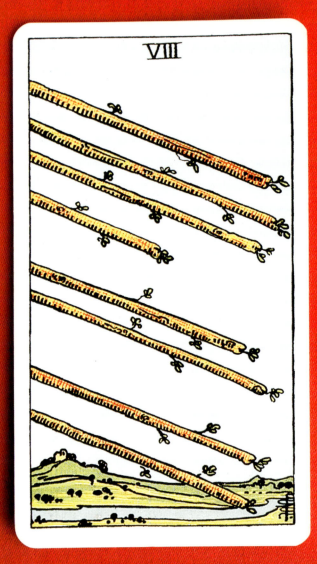

MINOR ARCANA

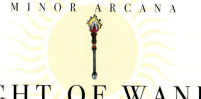

EIGHT OF WANDS

Eights represent movement and the Eight of Wands is the card of rapid speed. Hold onto your hats when this card appears as things are about to move very fast indeed. Things may feel a bit fast and furious with no grounding, so try to keep perspective. This card represents spontaneity and adventure and a sudden rush of energy. It affords the questioner the opportunity for a quick answer and often brings a fresh start.

INTERPRETATIONS

UPRIGHT

The on-the-go energy of this card may feel a little overwhelming, but try to see the opportunities that are being presented here. If faced with a lot of choices, see it as a positive, more information means better decisions. You may get sudden unexpected messages, or love that has been stagnant going into fast-forward. Whatever, you need to be ready for change – embrace it and enjoy the adventure.

REVERSED

Are you in flight mode? It is time to ground yourself and think about what it is you truly want. Get clear in your ideas. Alternatively, you may find plans being cancelled, people letting you down and not doing what they said. The energy feels stale and it seems like you have wasted your time.

MINOR ARCANA

NINE OF WANDS

This figure looks very weary, and is in a defensive stance. He may feel like giving up but somehow he will find the strength to carry on. He has been through a lot but is preparing to move on with new-found wisdom and a sense of self-awareness that may not have been there before. He obviously feels like he has something that is worth fighting for, otherwise why put up the defences?

INTERPRETATIONS

UPRIGHT
When the Nine of Wands shows up in a reading it is a reminder to look at where you have come from, to acknowledge your strengths and your weaknesses. Use your inner strength to see the potential and be aware of any challenges you may face. This is not the time to give up in whatever area of your life you are asking about. You may feel down, but you are not out.

REVERSED
Have you been so defensive that you have shut others out? Or are you feeling so overwhelmed by the opposition you are facing that you're just exhausted? Take into account your well-being when this card shows up reversed – there is no shame in asking for help or leaving a situation completely.

MINOR ARCANA

TEN OF WANDS

The figure in the Ten of Wands is carrying a heavy load, hunched over and struggling. The burden is almost too much for him. The thing is, he is not giving up, he is trudging along determined to carry that load to wherever it needs to go. The sense of determination is astounding at times. But does he need to carry that load all by himself, or could he maybe ask for help? Is he so used to carrying the burden that it is just normal to him?

INTERPRETATIONS

UPRIGHT

We can get overwhelmed by life's burdens and feel at times like everything is just too much. You may have been taking on more than you need to. When the Ten of Wands shows up in a reading, it is time to put some of that load down. Learn to delegate, ask for help or even let go of people who are dragging you down. Ask yourself, what are you holding onto that you could actually let go of at this time?

REVERSED

When the Ten of Wands is reversed it shows that the burden has become too much to bear. Something has to give but don't let it be your health or your mental well-being. It is okay to ask for help and it is probably necessary at this time. You don't need to feel guilty for needing some 'me' time.

MINOR ARCANA

PAGE OF WANDS

This messenger brings his youthful passion for life to a reading. Expect to be inspired and feel that spark of excitement entering your life when you see this page in a reading. He is fearless in his pursuit of all things new and interesting. His light-hearted energy comes with a sense of charm and confidence that encourages bold moves to be made. The Page of Wands brings you a message that adventure awaits.

INTERPRETATIONS

UPRIGHT

In a love reading, the Page of Wands encourages you to spice things up and relight the fire of passion. If it is a new interest however, it may be all passion with little chance of long-term sustainability. In careers, this page encourages you to take risks, find your passion and to not be afraid to make bold moves. If it hasn't already happened, expect some fresh optimism, fun and energy in your life. It is time to start living!

REVERSED

The page's childlike energy can be destructive. A reckless attitude towards situations may land you in trouble. Are you taking risks just to get an adrenaline rush? If the Page of Wands is reversed, you may be easily distracted by the next shiny object and not seeing things through to their conclusion.

MINOR ARCANA

KNIGHT OF WANDS

Although the Knight of Wands is more mature than the Page, he represents the extremes of the wand energy. He can be daring and adventurous, but this can lead to restlessness. He is charming but can be insensitive. But he does bring adventure and excitement to a reading. He is full of enthusiasm and is willing to take risks. Unlike the Page, his risk-taking is usually a little more thought-through. He is an extrovert, so buckle up, and be prepared for a good time.

INTERPRETATIONS

UPRIGHT

Passion and excitement are strong when the Knight of Wands appears in a reading. In matters of the heart, this may mean an exciting love affair but not one that necessarily lasts. But in other matters this passion is so ignited that you can expect to really have your lust for life at full-throttle. Whatever you do, when this knight is around, connect with your go-getting joyous energy.

REVERSED

When the Knight of Wands is reversed there is a good chance that he is being impulsive in some way. In love, he may leave just as fast as he arrived. There is a lack of follow-through and he appears to be unreliable, vain and quite insensitive. Reversed, this knight is too self-absorbed to notice who he burns in his wake.

MINOR ARCANA

QUEEN OF WANDS

The Queen of Wands is a beautiful, charismatic queen who knows exactly what she wants. The black cat at her feet shows that she is fully in touch with her feminine side. She is a magnetic individual, independent but loving. Although she doesn't care what people think of her, this queen will put you at ease and is life and soul of the party. When The Queen of Wands enters a room, all eyes are on her.

INTERPRETATIONS

UPRIGHT

When you draw the Queen of Wands in a reading you are being encouraged to embody her qualities. Embrace your sexuality, be confident in who you are and don't be afraid to shine. Your passion can take you to new heights. This queen is a leader who is definitely seen by others. Try new things, get adventurous with all areas of your life and see where your own personal joy can take you.

REVERSED

Reversed, we see the negative aspects of this queen. She is self-assured, but obnoxious and a total attention-seeker. If this is someone who is in your life, they may be over-shadowing you so much that you feeling invisible. The Queen of Wands reversed is a classic mean girl, gossiping and stirring up trouble just for fun.

MINOR ARCANA

KING OF WANDS

There is a vibrancy to this king that is like no other. Every man wants to be him and every woman wants to be by his side. He has such vitality and prowess that he is impossible to not be in awe of. The King of Wands exudes power and that fiery energy he brings can be a little bit intimidating to be around. He knows what he wants and he relishes the adventure of finding it. Although he can be a bit of a drama king, most people love him.

INTERPRETATIONS

UPRIGHT
Harness this king's energy by boldly going out and conquering the world, metaphorically speaking. He shows up when you are ready to learn from past mistakes and use them to inform your future. You understand what your limits are but you have gained a whole arsenal of new skills along the way. Basically, whatever you want to do, you can do it now. Commit to what you love and are passionate about.

REVERSED
Reversed, the King of Wands is off his game. You may have been over-confident and fallen flat on your face. Or someone may be holding you back because they feel threatened by you. Maybe you have an issue with authority that is making it hard for you to progress. This king can be a bully, so watch out.

Picture Credits

Alamy: 9 (Michael Honegger)

Dreamstime: 7 (Benjavisa Ruangvaree), 65 (Vieranika10), 85 (Mariia Petrova), 93 (Wieland Teixeira)

Dreamstime/Anna Denisova: 104/105, 134/135, 164/165, 194/195

Dreamstime/Vera Petruk: 6, 12 right, 17, 29, 45, 53, 57, 73, 81, 97, 101

iStock: 37 & 69 (Theasis), 77 & 102 middle (Vera Petruk)

Minneapolis Institute of Art: 12 left, 21, 33, 41, 49, 61, 89, 102 right

Shutterstock: 10 (Natalie Magic),12 middle & 25 (Evgenia Pichkur), 102 left (Vera Petruk)

Shutterstock/Roman Sibiryakov: 14, 18, 22, 26, 30, 34, 38, 42, 46, 50, 54, 58, 62, 66, 70, 74, 78, 82, 86, 90, 94, 98, 106-132, 136-162, 166-192, 196-222